JAMES GRANT

Bad Soil: So How Do You Show Up?

First published by Four Granted Publishing 2025

Copyright © 2025 by James Grant

All rights reserved. No part of this publication may be reproduced, stored or transmitted in any form or by any means, electronic, mechanical, photocopying, recording, scanning, or otherwise without written permission from the publisher. It is illegal to copy this book, post it to a website, or distribute it by any other means without permission.

First edition

ISBN: 979-8-9928323-0-3

This book was professionally typeset on Reedsy.
Find out more at reedsy.com

Contents

Bad Soil: So How Do You Show Up?	v
Introduction	vi
Chapter 1: The Illusion of Ownership	1
Chapter 2: Profit Is Pirates Without Bloodshed, and Pirates...	5
Chapter 3: The World of Pirates	9
This World Is Nothing But Pirates.	10
Even History Is Piracy.	11
Chapter 4: The Real Profit Is Your Attention	13
Chapter 5: Have Grace on Yourself	16
Chapter 6: The Four-Step Business Model & The Four Phases of...	20
Four-Step Business Model	20
Step One – Figure Out What Brings You Money	20
The Four Phases of Self-Realization	21
Phase One – Discovery	22
Chapter 7: The Four-Step Business Model & the Four Phases of...	24
Four-Step Business Model	24
Step Two – Get Some Money (or Whatever People Are Willing to Exchange for Their Time and Attention)	24
The Four Phases of Self-Realization	26
Phase Two – Action	26
Chapter 8: The Four-Step Business Model & the Four Phases of...	28
The Four-Step Business Model: Step Three – Pay People to Execute Step One (Efficiently)	28

The Four Phases of Self-Realization:	29
Phase Three – The Cocoon	29
Chapter 9: The Four-Step Business Model & the Four Phases of...	31
The Four-Step Business Model	31
Step Four – Refine and Repeat	31
Four Phases of Self-Realization	32
Phase Four – Flight	32
Chapter 10: Our Way Out and Moving Forward	34
Outro	38
About the Writer	39

Bad Soil: So How Do You Show Up?

by James Grant a.k.a. James Grant-Āyati

Introduction

There comes a time in everyone's life when they realize the world is not what they once thought it was. Some people come to this realization through hardship. Others experience it through education, travel, or deep introspection. Regardless of how it happens, there is a moment when the veil lifts, and we are faced with a question: *Now that I see things as they are, how will I show up?*

This book is not about easy answers. It is about the soil we have inherited—the conditions in which we have been planted—and the choices we make in response. Some soil is rich, nourishing, and full of potential. Other soil is barren, toxic, and resistant to growth. Yet, no matter where we find ourselves, we must ask: Do we accept things as they are? Do we try to cultivate something better? Or do we simply survive as best we can?

Throughout these pages, I will share experiences, observations, and hard-earned lessons about life under the pressures of capitalism, systemic inequality, and the pursuit of meaning. This is not a self-help book in the traditional sense. I won't tell you what to do or pretend to have all the answers. Instead, I offer you a perspective—a way of seeing the world that might help you find your own path forward.

Because at the end of the day, the soil may be bad. But you still have a choice in how you grow.

All I hope to do with this book is emphasize the difference between protecting people and preparing people.

My purpose is to prepare people. This isn't inherently good or bad to me because when a person finds their purpose, it transcends judgment—it simply *is*. Purpose embodies both yin and yang. Whatever it is, it can be used for good or bad. Purpose exists, and when you discover it, you just know—it's something you must do.

I don't expect anyone to walk my life's purpose with me. People may come along for the journey, but I can't be surprised if they don't. I don't expect them to. One thing I know for certain is this: my purpose doesn't need to be sold. I'm not here to convince anyone this book is good or useful. Writing this book is simply what I'm supposed to do.

And because of that, I've found peace.

I've found equanimity, and maybe I'm nearing nirvana for my soul, preparing to return my spirit to its origin. When I uncovered my purpose, I didn't create it, father it, or give birth to it—I simply found it. I could feel it, and I knew. That clarity brought me peace. The only discomfort came from doing the work. Now that it's done, I feel complete. I've closed my circle, my loop.

When you close your loop, you know. You know that from this point forward, continuing feels like repeating the same things over and over again. That's where I am now—closing my loop and finally expressing the thought that plagued me for years in a way that's coherent.

Before I could articulate it, this thought left me feeling aimless, with no motivation. The inability to define it brought me years of depression. But now that I've clarified my purpose, I understand my life. I see the path I've walked and the meaning behind the things I've experienced.

When you read this book, I hope you can feel the pain, longing, and resilience expressed in these songs:

Al Green's "How Can You Mend A Broken Heart" captures the yearning to overcome sorrow:

I was never told about the sorrow
And how can you mend a broken heart?
How can you stop the rain from falling down?
Tell me, how can you stop the sun from shining?...

Stevie Wonder's "These Three Words" speaks to the simplicity and power of love, even in the face of loss:

These three words
* Sweet and simple*
* These three words*
* Short and kind*
* These three words*
* Always kindle*
* An aching heart to smile inside.*

Kendrick Lamar's "Alright" carries the certainty of survival and hope, even in hardship:

Hard times like, yah!
* Bad trips like, yah!*
* Nazareth, I'm [messed] up*
* Homie, you [messed] up*
* But if God got us then we gon' be alright*

Michael Jackson's "They Don't Really Care About Us" channels rage at systemic injustice:
* Tell me what has become of my rights*
* Am I invisible 'cause you ignore me?*
* Your proclamation promised me free liberty, now*
* I'm tired of bein' the victim of shame*
* They're throwin' me in a class with a bad name*
* I can't believe this is the land from which I came*

I've been studying business since I was five years old. Back then, my mother let us charge our friends twenty-five cents to play on our Nintendo system. By the time I was nine, I was learning about commerce, buying leather goods in downtown Los Angeles and selling them to others.

As I got older, I expected to become independently wealthy through business. But I didn't. I used to wonder why I wasn't succeeding—why I wasn't "good at business." Now I understand. What I was missing is something I'll define in Chapter 2, and this realization has brought me peace. I wasn't failing at business. I was failing at being a good capitalist.

It's my hope that by reading this book, more common people will gain clarity. When you truly understand the way the world operates—its harsh truths and flawed systems—you can begin to thrive, even in bad soil. Survival, both emotional and physical, is possible when the majority becomes as informed as the minority.

Chapter 1: The Illusion of Ownership

We like to believe that we own things. Property, businesses, land, even our own bodies—we attach so much of our identity to the idea of ownership. But if we take a closer look, we start to see that ownership is often an illusion, a construct designed to maintain systems of power rather than a fundamental truth of existence.

Think about it. From the moment we are born, we enter a world shaped by rules we did not create. We inherit systems of law, economics, and social structures that dictate what can and cannot be owned. But history shows that ownership has always been a fluid and often violent concept. Land is taken, resources are claimed, people are exploited—all under the banner of ownership.

But what does it really mean to own something? If you stop paying for your house, the bank takes it. If you can't afford healthcare, your body is subject to the whims of an industry more focused on profit than well-being. Even in business, entrepreneurs often find that what they "own" is contingent on market forces, investors, and legal loopholes that can strip them of everything in an instant.

Ownership, then, is not about possession. It's about control. And control is rarely in the hands of the people who do the actual living, working, and existing in these systems.

So how do we navigate this? If ownership is an illusion, what do we build our lives around? The answer is stewardship. Instead of trying to possess, we should aim to care for, nurture, and sustain. Whether it's a business, a community, or a simple plot of land, the question should not be, "How do

I own this?" but rather, "How do I care for this in a way that benefits more than just me?"

Understanding this shift is critical because once you stop chasing ownership for its own sake, you begin to see opportunities to build something deeper—something that cannot be taken away because it was never about possession in the first place.

But in order to break free from the illusion of ownership, we must first confront what ownership has evolved into under modern capitalism—profit. Profit is ownership in motion. It's the action of continuously extracting more value than what is given, the engine behind most of the systems we interact with daily. At its core, profit is simple: buy low, sell high. To move forward, we must fully understand this process and its grip on how we live.

Profit is buying low and selling high—no matter the angle or context.

The only requirement for profit is this simple equation: buy low, sell high. That's it. If something increases in value over time, all you need to do is buy it today and sell it at a later date when the value has risen. If something is cheaper in one place than another, profit comes from purchasing at the lower price and selling at the higher one.

Profit also happens when you create something once but sell it repeatedly—like a digital product or intellectual property. In this case, the aggregated revenue from multiple sales exceeds the cost of that single creation.

Profit can even arise from labor. If someone doesn't know the true worth of their work, you can profit by paying them less than the price at which their labor is sold. That, too, is a form of buying low and selling high.

Even when something decreases in value, profit can be made. If you can convince someone to pay a higher price now for something that will cost you less to acquire later, you're still engaging in the buy-low-sell-high dynamic.

No matter the situation, profit is always, in some form, the result of buying for less and selling for more.

CHAPTER 1: THE ILLUSION OF OWNERSHIP

Formally Defining Profit

I believe the best way to define something is by focusing on what it does, not what we call it. In *Thinking in Systems* by Donella H. Meadows, the idea is clear: systems are defined by their actions, not their labels.

With this in mind, profit is best understood as the action of buying low and selling high. This action-focused definition differs from more traditional definitions, which often treat profit as a noun. For example, according to *Dictionary.com*, profit as a noun is defined as:

1. **Pecuniary gain** resulting from the employment of capital in any transaction; the ratio of such gain to the amount of capital invested; returns, proceeds, or revenue, as from property or investments.
2. The **monetary surplus** left to a producer or employer after deducting wages, rent, costs of raw materials, etc.
3. **Advantage, benefit, or gain.**

When we look at profit as a verb, *Dictionary.com* defines it as:

1. To **gain an advantage** or benefit.
2. To **make a profit**.
3. To **take advantage** of a situation.
4. To **be of service** or benefit.
5. To **make progress**.

These definitions align with my central premise: profit is action-based. It is the continuous pursuit of buying low and selling high, whether in monetary terms, personal advantage, or progress.

Profit in Every Transaction

Every contract ever written is, at its core, a profit-seeking instrument. Every agreement, exchange, or transaction exists to extract as much value as possible from another party. At its foundation lies the principle of buying low and selling high.

Understanding this concept is critical, as it applies to every interaction—personal or professional. No matter how altruistic or transactional something appears, profit is always being sought. The form may vary, but the essence remains the same.

Chapter 2: Profit Is Pirates Without Bloodshed, and Pirates Are Profit With Bloodshed

Now that I've clarified that when I say "profit," I'm referring to the action of buying low and selling high, we can proceed to see the world of commerce for what it is: piracy.

Pirates steal whatever they see as valuable and don't want to pay for it. Pirates will also force you to take things you do not want and then rob you of everything you have. With the concept of "buying low" as a sliding spectrum, the lowest price anyone can pay for anything is zero—that is, to steal or take it. On the other side of an exchange, the highest price you can sell something for is everything someone has. In that case, you also have a pirate. So buying low and selling high are just two wings of the same bird—a bird that steals value on either end. Profit is pirates without bloodshed, and piracy is profit with bloodshed.

Now, let's not get too metaphysical or sidetrack with arguments like "pirates spend energy in the form of force to steal, so they're technically paying for it." Let's stick to the context of an exchange: what happens between two parties engaged in buying and selling.

The Watchmaker and the Pirate

With the analogy that "piracy is profit with bloodshed," I want to share a story that reveals how some capitalists got their wealth.

Imagine a master watchmaker in a trading town, crafting elegant, precise, and durable timepieces. This watchmaker never took on an apprentice, so the secrets of making these one-of-a-kind mechanical watches were theirs alone. Their reputation spread far and wide, and people knew the only way to get these special watches was to visit the watchmaker's shop in person.

Now, this is before the age of the internet, where you could verify someone's address with a quick search. Back then, if you wanted this watch, you'd need to make the journey yourself—by ship, train, or wagon—to the watchmaker's shop. The watchmaker, being modest, didn't advertise their greatness or put their face in public. Their work spoke for itself, and their customers spread the word. But this modesty created a vulnerability: no one really knew what the watchmaker looked like before arriving at the shop.

One day, a thief realized this vulnerability. The thief thought, *"If I break into the watchmaker's shop, kill the watchmaker, and take over their identity, I can sell all the watches and make a fortune."* And that's exactly what happened.

In the dead of night, the thief murdered the watchmaker and took control of the shop. The thief sold the authentic watches for years, as the original watchmaker had left behind a significant inventory, crafted out of pure passion. Over time, the thief even learned just enough about watchmaking to be dangerous. When the inventory of authentic watches ran out, the thief thought, *"These watches aren't that special. I can just make some myself and no one will notice the difference."*

This could have worked because, like flipping a light switch, most people don't understand the intricate workings behind something—they only care if it works. But the new watches never lived up to the originals. The thief didn't have the same love for making watches. They didn't possess the secret techniques the original watchmaker had perfected through years of dedication. When customers complained that the new watches didn't perform or last as long, the thief always had excuses:

CHAPTER 2: PROFIT IS PIRATES WITHOUT BLOODSHED, AND PIRATES...

- *"The materials are no longer available."*
- *"Lasting long isn't as important as having the latest design."*

The truth was simple: the thief didn't love making watches. They just wanted to profit.

The original watchmaker would have made watches for free because they loved the craft. They spent countless hours mastering their art, creating something exceptional. This mastery came from a lifetime of dedication, something only possible for someone passionate enough to invest every moment into perfecting their work.

The Egyptian Pyramids and Stolen Identities

Now, let's fast-forward to the 21st century and consider the pyramids of Giza. These massive stone structures are marvels of engineering, yet no new pyramids have been built in modern Egypt. Why is that? Did the ancient Egyptians suddenly stop building pyramids? Did they lose interest? Did they forget how?

I'd argue that a pirate—metaphorically speaking—stole the identity of the Egyptians. They profited off the reputation of the culture but couldn't replicate its achievements.

Think about it: you can't accidentally build something as great as the pyramids. They required love, passion, and mastery. If the people who built the pyramids loved doing so, they wouldn't have stopped unless something—or someone—stopped them. When something extraordinary ceases to exist, we should question the current occupants and dig deeper into the story.

The lesson here is simple: whether it's watches or pyramids, when greatness disappears, we should always ask: *What changed? Was it stolen? Was the original passion lost?*

Whether it's watches or pyramids, nations or sciences the same pattern emerges. The real creators—the ones who master their craft—work for the love of it. The ones who come after, who only care about profit, struggle to keep the illusion alive.

BAD SOIL: SO HOW DO YOU SHOW UP?

And when they fail, they rewrite history to make us believe that what was once possibly *never really existed at all.*

Chapter 3: The World of Pirates

All I hear is pirates. All I see is pirates. Therefore, all we are left with is a choice: scam with the scammers or suffer being scammed.

The Convenience Store Exchange

Imagine the world as a giant 7-Eleven convenience store filled with sweet things. You're a young person walking into this store looking for something sweet. "Sweet" is relative—it could be a car, a house, an education, clothes, food, a video game, or even a candy bar. You know this store has sweet things, so you go in and spot a Snickers bar. You grab it, walk to the clerk, and put down a $100 bill.

Now, the clerk looks at you—confused at first as to why you're using a hundred-dollar bill to buy a candy bar that costs two dollars. But as they size you up, they realize you don't seem to understand how the system works. They see an opportunity. Instead of giving you $98 in change, the clerk gives you two dollars and says, "Thank you for coming by. It was a pleasure doing business with you. Hope to see you again soon."

You're not fully aware of what just happened. The clerk seems pleasant, so you don't think anything of it. You take your candy bar and the two dollars and leave.

In this exchange, who is at fault? Are you, the young person, at fault because you didn't know how to count your change? Maybe because you were never taught about financial exchanges?

Let's step back. Imagine you went through 12 years of school, from ages

5 to 17, but weren't taught the essential skills you'd need as an 18-year-old adult to make sound financial decisions. You may have learned how to read and count, but no one taught you about budgeting, compound interest, loans, or financial systems. You weren't taught any laws, but if you break one, you'll be tried as an adult. You weren't taught how things are made, so you don't understand the value of objects—just that they appear and disappear, like items in Minecraft.

On the other hand, the store clerk—the owner of the store—knows exactly how money works. They could have given you the correct change, but they prioritized profit over fairness. If you don't see this clerk's actions as wrong, then you might not want to keep reading this book.

I liken the candy bar example to predatory loans, exploitative credit card practices, or paying small amounts of interest on large purchases over long periods of time. It's the equivalent of buying a $2 candy bar for $98 because the person or institution profiting from you could have done the right thing but chose not to.

This World Is Nothing But Pirates.

Every system, organization, and institution has been designed to make piracy more acceptable, palatable, and efficient. But we didn't get here willingly.

The world has seen many leaders try to wake people up to the harm being done—often by their own kind—but no one listened. Those leaders were silenced or killed. As someone with an MBA focused on marketing and finance, I've learned about all these financial instruments, institutions, and businesses. To me, they're just euphemisms for ways to cheat in the game of Monopoly.

Is Intelligence Just Cheating Smarter?

Is intelligence now measured by how well you follow the crooked rules that allow the mega-rich to extract value from everything else? Is that "smart," or is it cowardice?

CHAPTER 3: THE WORLD OF PIRATES

I don't know anymore. I've spent my entire life trying to build generational wealth because being poor in America sucks. I thought wealthy people were playing fair, so I tried to emulate them as a good, honest person. But business school showed me otherwise.

I learned in accounting and corporate finance how businesses see labor—not as people but as cost margins to control. I learned in marketing how to manipulate customers into making decisions against their own interests. In financial engineering, I saw the sheer audacity of how the wealthy cheat while feeding the rest of us a different story.

But it's not just businesses. Everything in this world is pirates in disguise—hiding behind the mask of well-intentioned humanity. Wealthy people and their institutions have been stealing from others since the days of the pyramids. Once they've stolen enough, they create laws to keep anyone from taking it back.

Even History Is Piracy.

Pirates have existed throughout history. In the Bible, the so-called "promised land" was already home to other people with families and communities. Yet, it was taken by force. Today, thieves and pirates are still winning, constantly rewriting the rules to suit their needs.

They create euphemisms to justify theft, and we unconsciously adopt these terms without questioning what they really mean:

- "Equity" means "the percentage of your whole I'm going to take."
- "Taxes" mean "what I'm going to take from what you've gathered."
- "Interest" means "what I'm going to take from what I gave you."
- Even "archaeology" means "what I'm going to take once I find it."

These systems are all built on one-way extraction. The idea of a "win-win" scenario is a fantasy capitalists create to mask what's really happening.

Until we acknowledge what we're seeing—that rich people are taking things they had no hand in making—humanity doesn't stand a chance. Many capitalists will even resort to force if people refuse to comply with agreements that prioritize the pirates' profit over fairness.

Whether it's a candy bar, a loan, or an entire system of governance, the same principles apply. You're either the pirate or the one being pirated. The question is: What are you willing to do about it?

Chapter 4: The Real Profit Is Your Attention

The profit capitalists truly seek isn't your money—it's your attention. With your attention consumed by survival, they're free to focus theirs on maintaining control.

Imagine the world as a vast desert, its floor crawling with stinging scorpions. You're stranded in the middle of this desert, standing on a small rock, desperately wielding a stick to fend off the relentless swarm of scorpions. These scorpions represent the spectrum of human treatment: at one end is kindness, and at the other, mistreatment.

But in this desert, kindness doesn't mean compassion or care. Kindness simply means not getting stung. Mistreatment, on the other hand, is the sting itself. The only way to avoid mistreatment is to keep swinging your stick, fending off the endless wave of scorpions.

Your stick represents money. For most people, money comes from work—usually for someone else. Society subtly coerces us into this cycle by exploiting the extremes of this kindness-mistreatment spectrum.

Breaking Down the Desert:

- **The Scorpions**: These represent threats of mistreatment. The more money you have, the better you can keep them at bay.
- **The Stick**: This is your willingness to work—often driven by pressure or fear.

Here's where the complexity begins. Some people don't just use their sticks to defend themselves—they hire others to swing sticks for them. Employers convince workers that they're fending off scorpions for their own survival. But in reality, employees are defending the employer's rock. The people at the top of the rock—the wealthy—never actually feel the scorpions' sting. They are too far removed, shielded by layers of others doing the hard work below.

Some people give up and let the scorpions sting them, understanding that while the stings hurt, they aren't always fatal. Occasionally, someone swinging their stick will take pity on others covered in scorpions and knock off a few—but these individual efforts barely dent the overwhelming swarm.

Others see someone beating off scorpions and assume that person's life must be easier. They try to climb onto someone else's rock or borrow their stick, thinking it will provide relief, not realizing that everyone is in the same desert, fighting the same battle.

The Desert of the Mind

This entire desert exists because we've been conditioned to believe it's real. The scorpions thrive because we've accepted that their presence is inevitable. We've been conditioned to believe this desert is reality—that this is the way things must be. We've turned the paradise of Eden into a barren wasteland in our minds. And while it's easy to blame the scorpions, they aren't the real enemy. The real problem is our collective belief that this desert is unchangeable, but the truth is the desert can change. It's a construct of human belief—a collective illusion that we've internalized and perpetuated.

Most capitalists didn't build their wealth by swinging their sticks harder than everyone else. They built it through theft. Resources in this desert are limited, and capitalists have always found ways to take what others worked to create. There are too many examples of capitalists who built wealth by taking advantage of limited resources while convincing the rest of us that we can fight our way up too if we just keep swinging. The problem isn't the scorpions—it's our belief that we have to fight them forever.To escape this endless cycle, we don't need to swing our sticks harder—we need to terraform the desert by changing our beliefs and reimagining what's possible.

Why Capitalists Seek Your Attention

Attention is focus sustained over time. Your attention is their greatest treasure—because when they have it, you're too distracted to notice them quietly taking more. Capitalists don't just want your money—they want your attention because attention is power. With your attention locked on survival, you're less likely to notice the ways they manipulate and control you.

Money itself is an abstraction. Consider American currency, for example. It's a token adorned with the faces of dead white men who profited from slavery, systemic oppression, and cruel systems of exploitation. Is it any surprise that white men, or their descendants, hold more of this token than anyone else? Why would they create something with their likeness on it only to allow others to amass it in greater quantities?

But it's not the paper bills that matter to capitalists—it's what those bills represent: control. Money allows them to dictate what you do and where you direct your attention. The paper bills grant the holder ability to direct your actions—to force you into doing things you wouldn't choose to do on your own. Without those tokens, you face the judgment and mistreatment of society, which has been conditioned to view financial struggle as a personal failing rather than a systemic issue.

The ultimate goal of capitalism isn't to accumulate tokens—it's to keep you trapped in a feedback loop of survival. As long as your attention is consumed by swinging your stick and fending off scorpions, you won't have the time or energy to reimagine the desert—or to envision a world beyond it.

But here's the truth: you don't have to accept this desert as your reality. The scorpions only have power because we believe they do. When we shift our focus from fighting them to transforming the desert, we take the first step toward freedom.

Chapter 5: Have Grace on Yourself

I've been growing a young mango tree for about three years now, and as of this writing, it's only 18 inches tall. Under normal conditions, a mango tree should grow about five feet per year, eventually reaching anywhere from 30 to 100 feet tall. But my mango tree isn't growing in normal conditions.

It's living in an 8.5-inch round, 3.5-inch deep glass vase filled with a hydroponic medium called lightweight expanded clay aggregate, or LECA. LECA is great for growing certain plants like lettuce, chard, and other greens in water without soil. Trees, however, don't thrive in water.

This isn't a special miniature mango tree. It's just a regular seed from a yellow or red mango, the kind you'd find in a grocery store. That seed is genetically programmed to grow into a towering, fully mature mango tree—potentially as tall as 100 feet. So, should I blame my mango tree for not reaching its full potential? Should I hold it accountable for not becoming what it was "meant" to be?

Of course not. What's holding it back isn't the tree itself—it's the environment I've placed it in. There's nothing inherently wrong with the tree. It's doing the best it can within the limitations of an 8.5-inch vase filled with water and the occasional dose of nutrients. It's showing up as a mango tree, expressing its nature as best as it can under the circumstances. I have no doubt that if I were to transplant it into rich, fertile soil, it could grow into the massive tree it's destined to be—assuming its growth isn't cut short.

You, as a human being, are no different. You were born with DNA containing everything you need to grow, learn, and evolve. But just like my mango tree, you may be planted in bad soil. You're growing as much as

CHAPTER 5: HAVE GRACE ON YOURSELF

you can in the environment you've been given.

Bad Soil Bad Outcomes

Think back to the analogy of the stolen legacy of the watchmaker and the scraps left behind, or the desert filled with scorpions and sticks. Both represent bad soil. Capitalist pressures, trauma, and the coercive stimuli we face daily? More bad soil. Whatever your response to these conditions has been, know this: it's okay. You've been doing the best you can under the circumstances.

It's important to recognize this: what you *do* in response to your environment isn't the same as who you *are*. What you do in response to this bad soil is not who you are. Your job, your behavior, and your outward expressions are not your true self—they are reflections of the environment your seed has been planted in. If your soil is a desert, survival tactics are to be expected. Your true identity requires the proper soil. Who knows what you could become if you were planted in a nurturing environment?

Grace Starts with Understanding

The key to having grace for yourself is recognizing the difference between showing up as something and identifying with something. For example, my expression as an electrician isn't who I am at my core. It's simply how I've responded to the trauma and pressures of capitalism. If I had different inputs—a different environment—I might express myself very differently.

Life is a series of inputs and outputs.

Life is inputs and outputs—it's that simple. We get out what's been put into us. This clarity has brought me peace because now I can see why things are the way they are. The broken homes, failed relationships, and silent violence we see in the world are outputs of the toxic inputs we've received. You can't get peace from violence. You can't get love from rape. You can't get cooperation from coercion.

So how can we expect humans to grow into compassionate, caring beings under these conditions? Yes, there will always be exceptions. As Tupac wrote, some roses grow from concrete. Two mango trees in my collection even seem to thrive in water. But these exceptions only prove the rule. It took hundreds of mango seeds for me to get those two outliers. Their survival doesn't mean water is ideal for mango trees. It only highlights the truth: mango trees grow best in good soil.

Humans are no different. Every now and then, we get a Martin Luther King Jr. or an Albert Einstein—extraordinary individuals who rose above the limitations of bad soil. But when most of our environment produces depressed, disconnected humans and narcissistic behaviors among the influential, it's clear that we're not thriving. Humans, like mango trees, don't grow well in bad soil.

The State of Our Soil

We live in a world where you can often make more by doing less. That's bad soil. Pirates and thieves are just weeds growing out of it. The virtues we cherish—kindness, cooperation, love—can't grow in this environment. We create bad people because we have bad soil. It's as simple as that. And until the soil changes, we'll continue to get bad outcomes. But here's the good news: weeds can serve a purpose. If we let the weeds do their job, which is to grow tall fast and die quickly, they can cover the ground to prepare the soil for something better. If enough weeds grow and spread to cover the barren desert, they can become the ground cover that helps heal the soil. Weeds can be sacrificed for the soil's greater good, making room for better growth in the future.

A Moment to Breathe

This chapter is meant to help you breathe. To remind you that you're doing your best with what you've been given. The next chapters will provide tools to help you see what the pirates and thieves are doing—and, more importantly, how to stop it.

Your Mind Is Your Greatest Asset

Living in bad soil isn't all doom and gloom. The silver lining is that you still have your mind. The best way to use it is to focus on something meaningful—something that keeps it from wandering aimlessly. Always remember that

CHAPTER 5: HAVE GRACE ON YOURSELF

wherever you are in life, you're doing your best under the conditions you've been given.

In Chapters 6 through 9, I'll introduce two paths with four steps each:

1. **The Four-Step Business Model**
2. **The Four Phases of Self-Realization**

One path will reveal what business is and how it affects us. I'll give you a simple tool to recognize the tactics of the systems that take more than they give. I want you to be prepared, to have the knowledge to defend yourself. And I hope that by understanding these systems, you can stop them from controlling you. The business model reveals how the pirates and thieves manipulate you—and how you can begin to break free.

The other path will encourage you to discover your true identity, apart from what you currently show up as in this world of bad soil. Until you find your purpose, you'll keep showing up in response to the pressures and trauma of capitalism. But once you start to shift your focus, you can redefine your role. So, I ask again: *What's your response to bad soil?*

Everything comes back to balance—the yin and the yang, the beauty of circles and spheres.

Let's move forward.

Chapter 6: The Four-Step Business Model & The Four Phases of Self Realization

Four-Step Business Model

Step One – Figure Out What Brings You Money

The first step in building any business is simple: figure out how to gather money. This could be a service, a product, or a series of activities that consistently generate income. Keep it straightforward and focused.

Peter F. Drucker once said, "The goal of a business is to create a customer." A customer, in this context, is someone who willingly parts with their money. Your goal is to get as many customers as possible while convincing them to part with their money—ideally, as much as possible, as often as possible, and over a long period of time. But why create customers in the first place? Because without them, there is no profit.

Gathering money is about convincing people who have it—or control access to it—to give it to you. This isn't always about an even exchange. While traditional business assumes that customers pay for something they value, runaway capitalism has shown that profit doesn't always require delivering value. The goal is to ensure that money flows your way. Success, in this case, is measured by profit—how much of that money you actually get to keep after covering your costs.

The Two Pillars of Business Success

A successful business rests on two core actions:

1. **Gathering money:** The activities that directly result in people parting with their money and giving it to you.
2. **Keeping money:** The actions that reduce costs, inefficiencies, and leaks in your system so that you retain as much profit as possible.

Everything else—marketing, accounting, logistics—exists to support these two actions. Marketing helps you reach potential customers, accounting helps you track where your money goes, and operations ensure efficiency. But be careful not to confuse support activities with the money-gathering process itself. For example, improving your profit margin by reducing expenses is valuable, but it doesn't directly bring in new money. Identifying and refining the activities that generate revenue is key.

Turn Money-Making Into a Habit

Your goal is to develop habits that consistently generate money. To do this, you must be clear about the specific actions that lead to income. Once you identify those actions, structure your resources to support them at the lowest possible cost.

Ask yourself:

- What action convinces people to part with their money?
- What inconvenience, annoyance, or pain point can I solve that others are willing to pay for?
- How will I gather money, and how can I do it repeatedly?

The Four Phases of Self-Realization

Phase One – Discovery

The first step in self-realization is discovery, and it's often the most difficult. Discovery is about understanding what you truly want and clarifying your purpose. It requires self-reflection, honesty, and persistence. Many people struggle with this phase because their beliefs about what's possible are often limited by internal fears or external influences.

When we're told as children, "You can be anything you want," it sounds empowering. But without clarity about what we actually want, this statement can be paralyzing. We become overwhelmed by possibilities, unable to commit to any single path. This lack of focus leads to a scattered life, where we dabble in many things but master none because we never address the answer to "what do you want to do?"

Malcolm Gladwell's *Outliers* popularized the idea that mastery requires 10,000 hours of practice. But how can you reach that level of mastery if you're constantly switching from one pursuit to another? The discovery phase demands a commitment to one path. It's not enough to know you can do something—you must choose what you *want* to do and stick with it.

Dreams Require Determination

While it's true that you can achieve almost anything you set your mind to, that doesn't mean it will be easy. Pursuing your dreams requires determination and resilience. The discovery phase may take years, even a lifetime, but the effort is worthwhile.

Even if you never fully achieve your dream, the journey itself has value. The act of trying—of chasing what you're meant to do—can be more fulfilling than living a life of regret for not trying at all.

The Cultural Context of Dreams

As a Black person, I've seen how cultural and historical contexts can shape our relationship with dreams. For too long, Black Americans have faced systemic challenges that suppress aspirations. Even today, when a young Black person shares their dream, they may encounter skepticism, doubt, or discouragement—from their peers, their community, or society at large.

But we must push back against this conditioning. We need to allow ourselves to dream without limits. Speak your dreams into existence. Share them with others. Write them down. When you do, you might be surprised by how many people want to help make those dreams a reality. Dreams are powerful, especially in communities where hope has been systematically denied.

The Importance of Dreaming

Dreams aren't just for Black Americans—they're for everyone. Without dreams, you risk becoming a passive participant in someone else's vision. Don't let the world stifle your imagination. Your dreams are the foundation of your self-realization and the first step toward discovering who you truly are.

Dreams are seeds. They need the right environment, care, and attention to grow. And once they start growing, they can lead you to the next phase of your journey. Keep dreaming, and don't be afraid to dream big.

Chapter 7: The Four-Step Business Model & the Four Phases of Self-Realization Continued

Four-Step Business Model

Step Two – Get Some Money (or Whatever People Are Willing to Exchange for Their Time and Attention)

Now that you've figured out how to gather money in Step One, it's time to actually start getting some. Ideally, you'll begin generating income by performing the action(s) you identified in the previous step. This stage serves as a proof of concept and helps you build the funds necessary for the next phase.

However, if you're not yet ready to make money through your chosen activities, you'll need to raise capital to support your efforts. This step involves two key components:

1. **Creating a Start-Up Budget**: Determine how much capital you need to kick things off, including operational costs, marketing, and any tools or supplies necessary to sustain your money-making activities.
2. **Raising the Capital You Need**: Identify where your funding will come from and pursue those sources strategically.

Sources of Capital

1. **Savings**

If you have savings, this is your most straightforward option. Self-financing shows commitment and belief in your idea, which can make it easier to attract additional support down the road.

1. **Friends and Family**

Friends and family should be your first external resource. Convincing them is excellent practice for more challenging funding sources. Their support typically comes with fewer conditions, but don't take it lightly. Treat their investment as seriously as you would any other.

1. **Crowdfunding**

Crowdfunding requires creativity and marketing. You'll need to craft a compelling story that resonates with a broad audience, demonstrating why your project deserves their support. Success in crowdfunding hinges on your ability to sell your vision.

1. **Investors**

Investors can be a powerful funding source, but they come at a cost. Most investors are pirates, and if you lack leverage, you may be forced to give up more equity than you're comfortable with. Understand the risks—giving away too much control could cost you your long-term vision.

1. **Debt**

Taking on debt is another option, but it comes with obligations like interest payments and repayment schedules. To secure a loan, you'll typically need proof of income or assets as collateral. Be cautious and have a repayment plan in place to avoid financial pitfalls.

The Four Phases of Self-Realization

Phase Two – Action

Once you've discovered what you want to do, the next phase is to take action. But here's the catch: this phase can be just as difficult as discovery, if not more so. When you start making moves toward your dreams, don't be surprised if friends, family, and even your own inner voice begin to cast doubt on your chances of success.

Overcoming Barriers

When you know your purpose but feel stuck, ask yourself: *What's holding me back?* Identifying obstacles is the first step. From there, you need to find ways to go over, under, or through them. If you don't take action, you're making a choice—a choice to do nothing. And that's a decision you'll carry with you.

Consider the alternative: living a life dedicated to making other people rich. How are you supposed to feel fulfilled when you're stuck working for someone else's gain? The truth is, you're not supposed to feel fulfilled. If you're pretending to be excited about it, you're fooling yourself and that's okay. The system wasn't designed for your joy; it was built for profit, and capitalism doesn't care about your happiness.

But here's something important to remember: participating in capitalism doesn't mean you have to believe in it. Showing up as one thing while identifying with something else entirely is possible. This duality allows you to navigate the system while working toward your true goals.

The Power of Deliberate Action

Whatever you truly identify with—whether it's your purpose, your creative passion, or your entrepreneurial vision—achieving it will require deliberate choices, sacrifices, and consistent action. Pirates and thieves have no interest in helping you succeed, but they also can't stop you if you're determined.

When you take control of your actions, you take control of how you show up in the world. Yes, the system is rigged in favor of the pirates, but your choices, persistence, and intentional efforts are how you reclaim your agency. Keep moving forward, and let your actions define you—not the system.

Chapter 8: The Four-Step Business Model & the Four Phases of Self-Realization Continued

The Four-Step Business Model: Step Three – Pay People to Execute Step One (Efficiently)

You don't have a business system until you have at least one person performing the activities you identified in Step One (from Chapter Six) and you directly benefit from their work. The dynamic of paying others to execute your money-gathering system lies on a spectrum: at one extreme is slavery, and at the other is partnership, with traditional business practices occupying the middle ground as an exchange-based system.

In a world where people are often trapped by their need for money, your role as a business owner is to leverage that need as an incentive. You hire individuals to trade their time for money, performing tasks that, in turn, generate revenue for your business. To ensure profitability, your goal is simple: the value generated by the people you pay must exceed the cost of paying them. In essence, you "buy low" (by paying labor efficiently) and "sell high" (by ensuring that labor drives revenue).

Even if your business generates significant revenue, it won't succeed without profit. Money loses value over time due to inflation and other economic factors, so profitability is essential for sustainability. That's why it's crucial to minimize labor costs while maximizing output. This balance is at the heart of business success: you need to pay people efficiently while ensuring their work contributes to your bottom line.

However, keep in mind that the extremes of this balance can lead to ethical questions. At one end, exploiting labor too severely reduces morale and productivity, potentially harming your business in the long run. On the other end, paying too generously without ensuring returns could jeopardize your profitability. Walking the fine line between these extremes is how successful businesses sustain themselves over time.

The Four Phases of Self-Realization:

Phase Three – The Cocoon

Not being where you want to be in life isn't always about what you're not doing—it's often about what you are doing that's holding you back. For much of our lives, we move like caterpillars—slow, deliberate, and focused on immediate tasks. But at a certain point, forward motion requires us to stop, reflect, and shed the habits, behaviors, or beliefs that are no longer serving us.

Imagine standing in front of a room filled with people, handing each of them a twig, and asking them to snap it in half. When they ask why, you explain: "Sometimes we aren't where we want to be in life because we're holding on to the wrong things. Breaking the twig symbolizes breaking free from limiting habits, fears, and mindsets."

Stopping doesn't mean failure. *Stopping is progress.*

The cocoon phase is often misunderstood because, to the outside world, it appears as stagnation. People may assume you're stuck or failing. But just as a cocoon is a butterfly in transformation, this phase represents internal growth. Beneath the surface, you're evolving into something more powerful, capable, and efficient, even if that transformation isn't visible to others.

In Phase Two (Action), you moved forward as a caterpillar—slow, determined, and constantly learning from your environment. But as you gain knowledge and experience, you'll reach a point where doing things as a caterpillar won't get you to the next stage. That's when the cocoon phase becomes essential. While it may feel like you've hit rock bottom, this is simply a necessary pause for transformation.

The cocoon phase is uncomfortable. It's a time when progress seems out of reach, and self-doubt can creep in. But this is where the magic happens. It's in the stillness of the cocoon that you rewire your mind, shift your habits, and prepare for a breakthrough. When you emerge, you'll be a butterfly—capable of soaring with efficiency and grace. What once took hours of slow, deliberate crawling will now take moments as you move toward your purpose with newfound ability.

Embrace the cocoon. It's not a dead end—it's the beginning of your transformation.

Chapter 9: The Four-Step Business Model & the Four Phases of Self-Realization Concluded

The Four-Step Business Model

Step Four – Refine and Repeat

The final step of the business model is straightforward: repeat Steps One through Three, but with an emphasis on continuous improvement and refinement. This step is about eliminating activities that don't generate money, don't generate *enough* money, or aren't being performed efficiently. Replace them with tasks or processes that create greater profitability or align better with the strengths of your team.

As you cycle through these steps, you'll become more adept at focusing on the activities that directly contribute to revenue or cost savings. The goal is to maximize profit by ensuring that the value generated by your team exceeds the cost of employing them.

To achieve this, you must establish clear metrics to measure the return on investment of the tasks you're paying for. When certain activities fall short, you have options: improve them, reduce their associated costs, or eliminate them entirely. This refinement process is how businesses scale—by optimizing systems to achieve maximum efficiency and profitability.

Four Phases of Self-Realization

Phase Four – Flight

The flight phase represents mastery. In this stage, we do many of the same things we did as caterpillars—moving forward, gathering resources—but now, as butterflies, we are far more efficient and purposeful. As caterpillars, we simply consumed and left waste. Now, we pollinate the same environments we once extracted from, leaving behind vibrancy and value. Our presence doesn't just take from the world—it enriches it.

Obstacles that once loomed large as roadblocks are now minor challenges we can fly over. The casual observer who may have doubted us during our cocoon phase now sees us soaring, our progress measured not in inches or feet but in miles. Our perspective has completely transformed—we can see where we are, where we're going, and where we want to be, all at once. This clarity fuels our confidence and enables us to accomplish meaningful goals while providing solutions we couldn't even comprehend as caterpillars.

No longer are we left with scraps or leftovers from the world around us. We now choose the best resources and opportunities, selecting what we want rather than settling for what remains. This is what preparation leads to. This is the result of training, deliberate practice, and deep learning. Transformation isn't just about becoming something different—it's about becoming better equipped to live purposefully and efficiently.

We know we've overcome the cocoon phase when everything starts to feel aligned. It might seem as though the universe is conspiring in our favor, helping us bring our dreams to life. While it's tempting to attribute this shift to cosmic forces, the truth is more grounded: our internal changes manifest in external movement, and that movement creates alignment with the people and opportunities around us.

The Three Types of People in Flight

As we soar toward our goals, we encounter three types of people:

1. **Those who help us.** These individuals are aligned with our direction, actively supporting our growth and success.
2. **Those who hurt us.** These people are in opposition to our goals and may slow us down or create obstacles.
3. **Those who do nothing.** These individuals aren't aligned with us in any way, and their inaction has no effect on our path.

It's vital to identify the people in the first two categories. Those who help us deserve our attention and appreciation because their alignment accelerates our progress. Conversely, those who actively work against us must also be recognized—not necessarily to oppose them, but to understand their influence and mitigate their impact. Interestingly, those who do nothing can often be the least concerning because their lack of action neither helps nor hinders us.

These three archetypes of human behavior have existed throughout our lives, even if we didn't always recognize them. What matters most is learning to navigate these dynamics intentionally. As we soar, our ability to align with helpers, navigate around hinderers, and move forward despite bystanders becomes the key to maintaining momentum and thriving in the flight phase.

Chapter 10: Our Way Out and Moving Forward

Knowing what's wrong with the world doesn't automatically untrap us from the circumstances we face. Change can't happen in isolation—it requires a shift in the entire system and its cycles. I believe this idea is brilliantly encapsulated in Arthur C. Clarke's novel *Childhood's End*. While I won't spoil the book for those who haven't read it, its central relevance here is the necessity of humans outgrowing childlike behaviors.

What Are Childlike Behaviors?

One of the most persistent childlike behaviors is the belief in ownership. Think deeply about it—how can we truly "own" anything beyond the thoughts that come from our minds, and even then, only without the use of force or restriction? Ownership is merely a euphemism for control, exclusion, and dominance.

We grow up when we accept that we cannot own anything. We mature when we recognize that we are made entirely of the earth—assembled from the food and water consumed by our mothers, sparked into life by forces beyond our comprehension. And the earth itself, hurtling through space, is not stationary; it's in perpetual motion, orbiting a star, which itself is part of a larger celestial dance of galaxies.

Imagine being born into this universe—on a planet speeding through space like a convertible on a rocky road—and declaring ownership over anything.

CHAPTER 10: OUR WAY OUT AND MOVING FORWARD

Picture a newborn baby crawling out of the womb, opening its eyes, and immediately announcing, "I own you," to its mother, to the doctor, and to everything it sees. All of this while that newborn's very existence is occurring on a moving truck, driving on a container ship, navigating a turbulent ocean under a burning ball of fire in the sky. That is what humanity looks like when we declare ownership over the earth, the very entity that gave birth to us.

The Sick Ego

Ownership isn't the only childlike behavior that holds us back. Once people believe they can own things, they inevitably start to believe they are better than those who own less. It's one thing to notice differences between people, but it's entirely different—and dangerous—to create systems that reinforce superiority based on ownership.

We live in a world dominated by sick egos—people who find joy in exploiting the disadvantaged, competing against those who have no chance of winning, and laughing at those they've already defeated. These egos are like adults racing children, knowing full well they'll win, and still demanding applause for their victory.

What does it prove when an adult outruns a child? What does it demonstrate when someone with immense resources outcompetes those with none? It's not a fair game—it's a rigged system. The rich keep getting richer, then mock the poor for not catching up. They act as if the playing field is level, ignoring the fact that they've had an immeasurable head start.

This is what the wealthy do in narcissistic capitalism. They exploit, dominate, and then present their cruelty as kindness. When an employer pays us for our labor, they aren't being kind—they're simply not stealing all of our labor outright. Profit, by definition, requires taking something from someone. Yet we're told to admire and emulate these behaviors, we've been trained to admire this process—to accept cruelty as a virtue, to see greed as ambition and exploitation as success.

The Illusion of Solutions

Capitalism doesn't solve problems—it profits from them. Take the air in Long Beach, California, for example. It burns my nose. Instead of addressing the pollution that causes the issue, capitalism sees an opportunity to sell me allergy pills. This pattern repeats itself endlessly: treating symptoms rather than solving root causes.

Our childlike behavior as a society has led us to create "solutions" that often cause more harm than good. We don't truly address anything—we just mask the problem, and in doing so, we allow the cycle to continue. The time to stop and wake up is now because we can't guarantee that any products or services sold to us will do or solve anything it advertises. But we can be certain that products and services are designed to make profit, and we are certain that profit means to take something from someone.

But what happens when it all falls apart? What happens when the system collapses under the weight of its own narcissism and greed?

Children Are the Answer

As a result of reading Octavia E. Butler's *The Parable of the Sower* and *The Parable of the Talents*, I've come to believe that when society collapses into chaos, the best way to judge character, sincerity, and merit will be by observing how people treat children.

In Butler's novels, the protagonist learns to trust or distrust people based on how they respond to children in danger. This, I believe, is a deeply reliable metric. Children are vulnerable by nature, and the way individuals, organizations, and entire societies treat them reveals everything about their true character.

Do they protect the children in their care? Do they educate them? Are the children healthy, safe, and nurtured? Or are they targets of abuse, neglect, and exploitation?

When children are mistreated, it speaks volumes about those responsible for them. If adults cannot care for the most vulnerable among us, how will they treat those who show any weakness?

This becomes an even sharper lens when observing how people treat children who aren't their own. At that point, their actions are stripped of personal bias, revealing their genuine values and instincts.

Moving Forward

We can no longer afford to operate under the delusion of ownership, superiority, and narcissistic capitalism. Our path forward requires maturity—an abandonment of childlike behaviors and a commitment to systems that nurture and protect rather than exploit and dominate.

Children are our best hope for change. They remind us of the importance of vulnerability, kindness, and genuine care. By learning to treat children well—not just our own but all children—we create a framework for a society that values humanity over profit.

This understanding gives us a reliable way to gauge character, sincerity, and morality. And it also gives us a way out: through collective care, maturity, and a willingness to dismantle the illusions that keep us trapped. We don't need to build a new world—we just need to grow up and reclaim what was always meant to be ours.

Outro

I hope you're not feeling too down.

It's clear that businesses are playing hot potato with the earth—passing responsibility around without ever truly owning it. They only acknowledge the metrics that serve their interests and act as if the rest of the consequences don't exist. This kind of thinking is lazy. We can't afford to fall into that same laziness—the kind that profit-seeking encourages, where doing the right thing is always someone else's job.

But we have an opportunity. We can bring joy back to the earth, and that joy will do what fear and ignorance never could: it will heal, inspire, and unify. That joy will inevitably drive out fear and ignorance. Fear and ignorance have been the primary tools of narcissistic capitalism, used to keep people complicit in the status quo.

I hope you've changed. I hope your perspective has shifted, and that now, you can't unsee what you've come to understand about the condition of the earth and the state of its people. Once you truly see the world for what it is, you gain something precious: clarity. And clarity is the first step toward creating change.

Let's move forward—together.

About the Writer

I was born on September 11, 1984, in Los Angeles, CA, to my mother, Florence Reed, and my father, James Grant. I grew up in Compton, CA, where I was homeschooled from ages 8 to 13 before returning to public school at Jefferson Middle School in Long Beach, CA. I later graduated from the California Academy of Mathematics and Sciences in 2003 and left Compton and Long Beach to attend the University of California, Irvine, as a Mechanical Engineering student.

During my senior year at UC Irvine, I pledged the historically Black fraternity Alpha Phi Alpha, Fraternity Inc. Unfortunately, my grades suffered, leading me to change my major to Anthropology, which allowed me to graduate in 2008. After a few unsuccessful attempts in the financial sector and declining an opportunity to attend New York Law School due to a DUI in 2009, I spent five years working at Wells Fargo Bank.

In 2015, I began a new path, joining the Electrical Training Institute of the International Brotherhood of Electrical Workers (IBEW) Local 11 in Los Angeles. Around the same time, I was accepted to the Drucker School of Management at Claremont Graduate University for a master's in Politics, Economics, and Business. Initially, my goal was to strengthen my competitiveness in the financial sector and become an actuary, but during my admissions interview, I was warned about the limited job prospects for that degree. Instead, I was persuaded to pursue an MBA—a two-year, $150,000 program—rather than the one-year, $70,000 degree I had originally considered.

I postponed my enrollment and continued my electrician apprenticeship until the last possible moment before accepting my place at CGU. Informing my training institute of my plans, I temporarily left my apprenticeship to pursue my MBA, with the understanding that I could return and continue where I left off. From August 2016 to May 2018, I completed my MBA with concentrations in marketing and finance, graduating in the top 10% of my class. However, after finding that job offers in my field came with disappointingly low salaries, I decided to return to my apprenticeship.

When I attempted to resume my training, I discovered that no record of my agreement to continue where I had left off existed. As a result, I was forced to restart my apprenticeship from year one, with my previously earned hours reduced from nearly 3,000 to just 2,000. I worked as a first-year apprentice again until 2021, when a job coordinator noticed that my pay rate was too high for a third-year apprentice. Upon further investigation, a letter was found confirming that I was supposed to resume at 50% completion rather than starting over.

I was advised to stop taking apprenticeship classes and instead focus on passing the California state electrician exam. If I passed, I would be advanced immediately. On December 6, 2022, I received my passing score, and by December 13, 2022, I officially became a licensed electrician in California with IBEW Local 11.

That is how I have navigated the pressures of capitalism. Along the way, I have started several businesses and lived through major life transitions, all of which have shaped my unique perspective on the world.

www.ingramcontent.com/pod-product-compliance
Lightning Source LLC
Chambersburg PA
CBHW070040070426
42449CB00012BA/3111